The Song of the Sparrow

Poems by Alison Stedman

Illustrated with photographs by John Stedman

THE LEPROSY MISSION
ENGLAND AND WALES

THE LEPROSY MISSION WORLDWIDE

Australia:	PO Box 293, Box Hill, Victoria 3128
Belgium:	Wolterslaan 41, 9110 St Amandsberg
Canada:	40 Wynford Drive, Suite 216, Don Mills, Ontario M3C 1J5
Denmark:	Pile Alle 3, 2000 Frederiksberg
England and Wales:	Goldhay Way, Orton Goldhay, Peterborough PE2 0GZ
Finland:	PB 160, 00211 Helsinki
France:	BP 186, 63204 Riom Cedex
Germany:	Hellerweg 51, 7300 Esslingen/N
Hungary:	Alagi ter 13, Budapest 1151
India:	Church of North India Bhavan, 16 Pandit Pant Marg, New Delhi 110 001
Ireland (North):	Leprosy House, 44 Ulsterville Avenue, Belfast BT9 7AQ
Ireland (South):	5 St James Terrace, Clonskeagh Road, Dublin 6
Italy:	Via della Repubblica 114, 10060 S Secondo di Pinerolo (To)
Netherlands:	Kooikersdreef 626, 7328 BS Apeldoorn
New Zealand:	PO Box 10-227, Auckland 4
Norway:	Viges veg 20, N-3700 Skien
Scotland:	11 Coates Crescent, Edinburgh EH3 7AL
Southern Africa:	P. Bag X 06, Lyndhurst, 2106 Johannesburg
Spain:	Calle Bravo Murillo 85, Madrid 28003
Sweden:	Box 145, S-692 23 Kumla
Switzerland:	Chemin de Réchoz, 1027 Lonay/VD
Zimbabwe:	PO Box BE200, Belvedere, Harare

International Head Office: 80 Windmill Road, Brentford, Middlesex TW8 0QH, UK

By the same author:
Faith, Hope, Love (New Wine Press 1987)

Published by The Leprosy Mission England and Wales 1991
Goldhay Way, Orton Goldhay, Peterborough PE2 0GZ
England

ISBN 0 902731 31 9

Photoset and printed by
Stanley L. Hunt (Printers) Ltd, Midland Road, Rushden, Northamptonshire

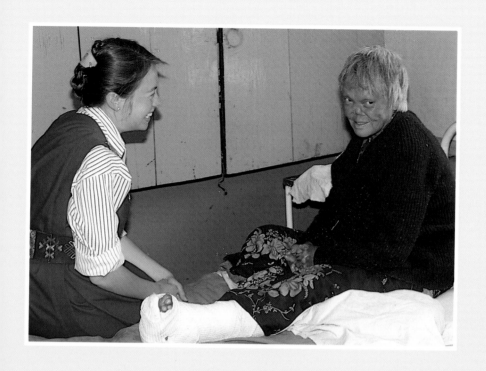

To all my
friends and colleagues
in Bhutan
especially those at
Gidakom.

Contents

KENSINGTON PALACE

I was very happy to be asked to provide a foreword for
is anthology of poems by Alison Stedman, a nurse working
th The Leprosy Mission in Bhutan.

Today there are more than ten million men, women and
ildren who continue to suffer the ravages of leprosy.
ring visits to Indonesia and Nigeria I have seen at first
nd the fortitude of those afflicted and the dedication of
ose who seek to help them. The Leprosy Mission is in the
refront of the battle against this disease and in bringing
w life to leprosy sufferers.

The poems in this marvellous book convey something of
e spirit of The Leprosy Mission's work and I warmly
mmend it to you.

Diana.

September, 1991

The Song of the Sparrow

I HAVE sadly neglected
Pouring colours of words onto paper
– but I mustn't lose it –
– mustn't let slip into silence
What You have poured into me!

Today,
One sparrow
Sat on the tight-rope of wire
Alone,
Against an open blue sky
And sang out . . .
As if knowing it had been created by You, God,
Given a voice to sing
Even into the vast empty blueness.

It wasn't afraid
But seemed to know
That God had counted it
Among His numbers.

And so I too
Must sing out
When I'm given a song!
Even if there is no-one listening
I must let notes
Fly . . .
With "one-a-penny" thoughts and words
To the creator
Of this sparrow,
– this sky,
– this song!

Dawn

THE glimmer of light
filtering through the curtains,
beckoned me to the window.
Soft grey-blue sky,
with traces of cloud
smudged along the mountains.
All was still.
A quiet, comforting feeling awoke inside
with the expectation of the day ahead —
a new beginning,
hope and future
hovered in this moment,
as night
tottered on the brink
of day.

Early Morning at Gidakom

AT first
all is still;
Time seems frozen in the morning frost
Each breath is echoed
in mists of water into the air.
Cold bites into our hands and faces
Making us shrink deeper
into layers of clothing.

Slowly the valley yawns
out of its lazy sleep,
Throwing back the mist and
Peeling off the night's cold blanket.

Ice-encrusted grasses soften and thaw
to the touch of the rising sun.
Streams of water run from roofs
White pillars of wood-smoke
Curl into the morning
A hazy veil
Suspending the clear white light across the valley
. . . gradually dissolves . . .
To reveal the mountains behind.

Dogs and children are the first to spill into the day.
While chickens busy themselves amongst the dirt.
Movement and warmth
percolate the icy stillness;
Quiet gives way to the day's busy hum.

Then the bell rings out to mark the day's beginning;
Calling us together
To hold the stillness for a moment longer,
Before The Creator,
As we offer ourselves and the rest of the day
    into His hands.

The Himalayas

(Previously published in *Faith, Hope, Love*)

THE morning light
   brings them alive
And they awake
In the golden browns and greens
   that adorn them by day.
Frost nestling in the valleys,
A scattering of snow
Gathered in the crevices,
− whiteness blending
With the clouds that shroud the tops from view.
These distant, majestic peaks
Shout to the world,
Pointing heavenward
   to their Creator −
You, who chiselled the mountains from the earth
And raised them up
To cut across the sky,
Towering above us
   in awesome splendour −
They reflect Your majesty.
As the sun sets,
The soft orange glow
Accentuates those craggy peaks,
And the dark shadow
Creeps down into the valley −
Until the blackness covers them −
Until the next morning
When they will
Shout again!

Mountain Rain

MOUNTAIN rain
Falls . . .
Pouring out its heart;
Skies bursting,
beating an angry fist against the earth!

Monotonous,
Pelting,
Hypnotic drumming
on the tin roof
. . . until the rhythm
becomes . . . endless noise!

Wetted stones
glint, freshly polished,
against lush greenness.

Grass and flowers
illuminated;
awakened into such clarity
of bejewelled dewy drops,
in a new-lit brightness.

Then the smell of earth
deep and full
rich and dark,
Fills the air;

Giving new hope and promise
to a wet afternoon!

Clouds

THE restless clouds,
Ever-moving
ride across the sky
or creep down
to sit in the lap of the mountains.

In bright sunshine
like icing-sugar crowns
they cover the peaks.

In dull wet drizzle
they hang . . .
like cobwebs
in the corners of the mountains;
curtaining the valley
to its eerie rain-filled fate.

So lace fine
you can't capture or touch
their delicateness.
Pearl misty droplets
escape your fingers
. . . and disintegrate;
leaving cold dampness
on hair and skin
like the trace of a dewy morning.

Then
there is nothing so beautiful
so magical
so distant or fleeting,
as a rainbow's painted colours
brushed across the whiteness
with a master stroke
from the promise-remembering
Creator!

The Ploughman

A PATCHWORK of layered fields
Stretch across the valley.
A farmer works
Steering the heavy plough
Through soft oozing mud;
Guiding the pair of sturdy oxen
Carefully, skilfully,
Around the curves,
So that each small field is tilled.

As I stand and watch
It seems I have stepped back in time.
This living history is painted before me,
Framed within the mountains and hung
        in the crisp still air.
It's the twentieth century
– the age of technology
    computers and space travel;
Yet here
the rush of the modern world
seems to have passed by, and
Time has paused!

Paddy Fields

HOOVED feet
tramp the dust
in an endless march;
Shoulders drag
a heavy wooden plough
turning over clods of rich soil.

Then the fields are flooded;
Hard steps
become shining miniature lakes,
layered mud-beds.

Finally
with skirts held up
tucked in tight belts,
backs bent
feet bare
legs wading through wet slime;
Busy hands
tenderly root
green rice-plants
deep into the murky soil;

Colouring in the valley
with the lush green promise of harvest.

A Prayer Walk

I FOLLOWED the butterfly
that kept alighting on the path ahead,
winking with opened wings
as if to say
"Follow me, I know the way".

Ripe grasses
bowed straw-pink heads
before a breeze
which stroked up the valley;

Invisible basking insects
hummed like an electric current.
Dragonflies on shimmering wings
skimmed through the air
like paper aeroplanes.
Checker-board butterflies
played chase, carefree,
rising like bon-fire ash
. . . up . . . up into the sky . . .

. . . Floating, soaring with them
my thoughts drifted,
my prayers reached up to You
offered up
like the fragrance of the pine trees.

Reassuringly
You answered me

"Yes, you've found The Way too".

A Journey Back from Thimphu

THE evening light
tucks folds
into the mountains.

These soft grey pleats
are the back-drop
to steps of emerald fields;
black and white timbered houses
reflecting gentle light
from grey-shingled roofs.

The valley lies bathed
in a serene beauty
Held in an image
of perfect stillness.

Serenade of Evening

THE evening hangs,
poised,
like a dusty cobweb.

Day slides
into restful night.

Echoes of a dog's bark,
the rush of the river's endless
sighing journey,
and a crickets' chorus,
Call
up into the sky,

Serenading the stars.

One Year at Gidakom

THE seasons have come full circle;
Dry browns and misty purples
Cloak the once green mountain sides again.
Blue skies emerge from heavy rain clouds;
White frosts chill the earth
Under clear starry nights.
The valley has yielded its harvest
To rough hands of busy farmers
Now leaving the ground to rest again.

Like the changing colours of the seasons
So our community has been
A patch-work of events —
Happiness, sadness,
Comings, goings,
Laughter and tears.
We have gathered in our harvest too —
A little more wisdom,
A greater depth of understanding,
And a lot more love
For this land
And its people.

"What Can I Say?"

CONVERSATION goes on all around me
Washing over my understanding.
Expressions and animated gestures
   give some meaning away,
         but
Like carefully guarded secrets
The packages of words
      stay hidden,
Like the mystery of an unwrapped parcel.

I answer with a blank stare and
   a questioning shrug
      "What did they say?"

The bridge of the third person
is often more of a barrier
– Interpreting my words,
in their tone of voice,
with their own emphasis,
– not mine!
Has my message really
reached its destination unchanged?
– I can never know for sure.

But the one thing
I can communicate
That I know is the same
in your language too

Is a smile!

His Touch

YOUR claw-like hands
and the sores on your deadened feet
Reach out
Crying for new life and purpose.

I want to answer you
in the warm language of touch
to say — "that you matter!"
        "that you are loved!"
        "that your life can be rebuilt!"

But you won't feel my hand
    you won't sense my touch
        — only numbness.
        — My touch alone is dumb!

So I pray —
    that deep down,
    deeper than your skin, flesh and bones
    You will hear the touch that says

— "Jesus loves you,

    He cares for you and
    longs to make you whole."
    Because my touch
    is given to you
    With His love.

Speaking Hands

THEIR hands say so much
Some cracked
Skin hardened,
Gnarled fingers curl like old twigs,
Ageing before their time.
Some are so twisted and clawed
   that they are trapped,
Locked in an angry fist.
Some are only stumps, dumpy and useless,
Eroded down like rocks in the path of a river –
Fingers seem to shrink away
. . . to nothing
As ulcers and burns take advantage
. . . of the numbness;
So gradually the natural tools of humanity
are destroyed.

Lord,
When we see your hands
There are scars there too
Left by our sins
They took hold of our pain willingly . . .
so that we could receive
Your healing touch of forgiveness.

Outcast

SOCIAL outcast,
Despised,
You wander from place to place
Not belonging,
Taunted and abused,
Spat upon.

People are afraid, embarrassed
To look you in the face.
You are taboo.
Abandoned by family and friends
Because you are different!

Your hands and feet bear the marks,
— but your scars go deeper.
Who knows what pain you bear?
    — Jesus —
He understands
Because He's been there too!

Isaiah 53:3-5

Tika Maya

TINY pinched face
Framed within wild matted bush hair.
Piercing hawk-determined eyes
. . . shout independence
Rebellion . . . at us!

Facing death with every laboured breath
Yet defying medicine
    and the law of patient-obedience.
— How do you make us feel?
How can you spit our care
Back into our faces!
We feel so angry . . . so helpless!
We try and get your body
To fight for itself
Against the disease that grips you,
While your fighting spirit
Makes us your target!

We see the poverty that binds you
And your bedraggled children
– this is your real enemy.
Why can't you see that?

We offer you our love,
Our care,
A cure!
But we can't bind you.
We can offer,
But we can't hold you captive!

– So you went
Like a cat back into the wild
To fend for yourself!
You struggled against us all the way;
You survived,
Leaving us wounded!

Glory and Suffering

A WORLD of contrast —

Vast beauty all around
Sun highlighting the magnificent
   mountains,
Dazzling blue skies,
Soaring eagles and
Delicate red dragonflies.

All shout to me of the Creator
The King of Glory!

But here too
Are sores and sickness
Sadness and pain;
Humanity with marred faces
hands twisted and worn away
feet crippled — left as stumps
Lives and nerves left numb
— useless.
All these whisper to me
of our suffering Saviour!

He reigns here
in the glory and the suffering!

A World of Difference

(Previously published in *Faith, Hope, Love*)

OUR eyes met
And for a few seconds
. . . Two worlds apart
Faced each other.

Standing with a pick in her hand,
And a sleeping baby tied to her back;
She stopped work for a few minutes.
Headscarf of faded cloth
Tied back dusty, uncombed hair.
Hands and feet leathered
From the constant work on the mountain
    road.

Snow lay around the shacks,
Icicles hung on bamboo walls.
A child was playing,
No nappy, no shoes.
Workers crouched round a wood fire,
Turned . . .
And met our gaze too.

What do you really think of us?
Foreigners,
Strangers
From another planet . . .
Called affluence
As we pass over your handywork,
Your toil and sweat.

She stared back at me,
How could I understand?
Not just a car window
Between us . . .
A world of difference!

A World of Difference – Again!

AGAIN I've seen
Into 'the world of difference'.

She came in grey thin pieces of cloth
With two children at her side,
Shadows of people;
Pinched old faces
In children's bodies;
Big eyes
– no anger
– no resentment
At our health and plenty;
– just tired acceptance.
Perhaps our eyes echoed
The anger for them!
Stunted growth with thin spindly legs
Tried to balance on the scales,
Wobbling like a new-born foal.

This time no car window
Between us
– that other world was standing before me
In bones and flesh.
Food, clothing,
Love and care were prescribed.

Lord,
Is this You standing here?
Is this the opportunity given
To feed and clothe You?
Do I hear You say
"When you do it for the least of these
    my children you do it for Me!"?

The Artist's Finest Work

HE had a sketch in mind
A plan
And so He created . . .
Sculptured mountains, lands,
Painted flowers, birds,
Sunsets . . .
Moulded man in His image
From the clay of the earth.

But

His finest work
Was as a carpenter
When He made a cross of wood
And gave His life upon it.
Those skilful hands
Were pierced
So that His life blood
Could flow,
Washing new colour,
Restoring His creation
To Himself again.

Now He waits
Poised
To add you,
To complete the picture.

I Am He

YOU stepped forward
You took our place,
You said "I am He".

The Alpha and Omega
The Almighty
The one they were looking for
The one they were waiting for,
Yet the one they came to arrest.

So they took You
and You let us
Go free!

John 18:2-9; Exodus 3:14;
Revelation 1:8; John 8:58

A Stumbling Block or Folly?

YOU hung from the tree,
A death so terrible
So foul,
That the curse of God had to be upon You.
And it was!
"So how could You be the Messiah?"
The Jews asked.
But You are . . .
And so to them
You are a Stumbling Block!

Human weakness
At its most vulnerable
— at the point of death.
No regal dignity there
And there wasn't!
"Where is the conquering King?"
The Gentiles asked.
But you are . . .
And so to them
You are only Foolishness!

So what is your conclusion
To the identity
Of the man at Calvary?

1 Corinthians 1:22&23;
Deuteronomy 21:22&23;
Galatians 3:13

In Whose Image?

THE sound of metal striking metal
rings out . . .
as the heat of the fire burns white hot,
and the melting pot bubbles.
With all his energy
the man works,
crafting each detail
into this small silver figure.
Each curve of the limbs —
each expression,
each poise of the hands —
he moulds and makes
for his worship and adoration,
born only from his imagination
— made in his own image!

Listen again,
to the sound of hammering . . .
metal hits flesh and as blood seeps into the wood
a man cries out in pain!
Look at the cross —
This is the way
that the Son of Almighty God
was crafted . . . completed,
as He surrendered all to His Father's will,
laying down His life for us.

This was His melting pot
Filled with pain, flesh, blood,
Love and Forgiveness.

From this He arose
an Eternal, Living God!
Not found in stone,
cold hard metal or
carved dead wood;
but living
with the beating pulse of His Spirit
that comes to let His image
be born again
in us!

Isaiah 44:6-20; Genesis 1:26&27

53

The Rise and Fall

JESUS
When the nails pierced Your hands,
Did you hear the Devil
laughing in Your ear?

When You hung there
aching . . .
with the weight of all darkness
on Your shoulders,
Was Satan's voice
ringing out in a loud victory cry?

When You lay
cold with death in the tomb,
Could You feel his fire burning fiercely
as he danced in triumph on Your grave?

Then,

When You went down
to claim the keys of sin and death,
Was there terror and disbelief
on his face?

When You rose
Victorious,
As The New Day dawned,
Could You hear his shriek of defeat?
Or was the beautiful chorus of angels
and rapturous applause of heaven,

So loud
That it left him speechless?

A Way of Seeing

OUT in front of me,
Stretching away to touch the sky,
lie the fields;
The valley
turns and folds,
buckling and tunnelling its way
between the mossy mountains.

Lord,

Would this view look the same to everyone
    who studied it?
Would each detail, each prayer flag,
    each farmhouse,
hold the same light?
Or do You make our seeing as individual as we are?

Would the sky look as blue
If I didn't know
that You had created it?
Would the greenness look so fresh
unless I knew
that it was Your dewy-rain
that had watered and nurtured
    each tree and plant?

Would the light seem so clean,
so warm, so bright,
If I didn't know that Your Light
Had come into this world
To shine in our hearts?!

Reverse Culture Shock

WAITING for the impact of
"Reverse Culture-Shock".
– but the culture was just the same
as I'd left it!
Waiting to be disgusted
by 20th Century life
– the noise
– the materialism
– the lack of concern for the outside world;
But I slipped back into it
All too easily,
Taking for granted what I'd always done
. . . or did I?
Blending into the crowd again
No longer the foreigner, the stranger.
Hearing and understanding everything going
on
around again
Belonging
. . . or do I?

So what's changed, what's new?
Yes – the children have grown,
And prices have gone up,
(especially when you think
    how many rupees it would be!)
And there are new adverts on TV.
The supermarkets have got bigger,
Brighter, more efficient.

— Fast Food, has got faster,
And there's so much more to choose from
. . . or is there?

The traffic has got noisier
The cars go much faster,
Exhaust fumes have got smellier
— it takes longer to cross the road
. . . or does it?

So who's changed
You or me?

We both have
But in different places
At different paces,
In different ways,
For different reasons.

Yesterday I was sitting
On a quiet mountain slope;
Yesterday I was bandaging
An ulcerated hand with a piece
Of old bed sheet;
Yesterday . . . I was there,
Today . . . I am here,
Back home!
. . . is this home?
Or am I just visiting?

Poetry

THE page is my canvas.
With simple words
and small strokes,
the images are traced out.
Things around and within
provide the design.

A feeling
– an emotion
to capture, to hold,
and reflect back;
to feed your thoughts,
stir your imagination,
provide the colour,
For your mind's eye to add the details
mine has left unsaid.

If you see the finished picture,
If the canvas is filled,
the vision completed,
hung treasured in your heart,
Then I am satisfied!

How Dark

HOW dark is it to be blind?

How silent is it to be deaf?

How cold is it to be dead?

How lost is it to be without Christ?

Alison Stedman

Alison Stedman was born in Plymouth in 1963.
She trained as a nurse at Guy's Hospital in London
and worked at St. Christopher's Hospice for two years.
In 1988 she went to Bhutan to work with
The Leprosy Mission at one of their hospitals.

These poems are a reflection of her life and work in that country.

John Stedman

John, Alison's father, taught with
Voluntary Service Overseas in Bhutan from 1984-87.
A keen photographer, he was much inspired with the beauty
of this small Himalayan Kingdom.
A selection of his photographs complement
Alison's verse in this anthology.